INSIDE THE NFL

Chicago Bears

BY
ZACH WYNER

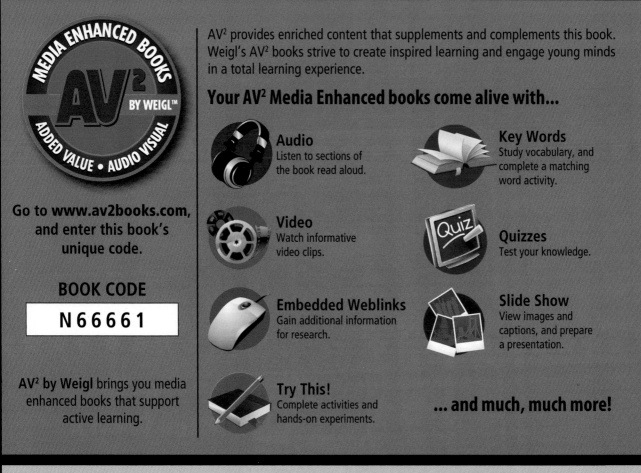

AV² provides enriched content that supplements and complements this book. Weigl's AV² books strive to create inspired learning and engage young minds in a total learning experience.

Your AV² Media Enhanced books come alive with...

Audio
Listen to sections of the book read aloud.

Key Words
Study vocabulary, and complete a matching word activity.

Video
Watch informative video clips.

Quizzes
Test your knowledge.

Embedded Weblinks
Gain additional information for research.

Slide Show
View images and captions, and prepare a presentation.

Try This!
Complete activities and hands-on experiments.

... and much, much more!

Go to www.av2books.com, and enter this book's unique code.

BOOK CODE

N66661

AV² by Weigl brings you media enhanced books that support active learning.

Published by AV² by Weigl
350 5th Avenue, 59th Floor
New York, NY 10118
Websites: www.av2books.com   www.weigl.com

Copyright © 2015 AV² by Weigl

Library of Congress Control Number: 2014930846

ISBN 978-1-4896-0802-4 (hardcover)
ISBN 978-1-4896-0804-8 (single-user eBook)
ISBN 978-1-4896-0805-5 (multi-user eBook)

Printed in the United States of America in Brainerd, Minnesota
3 4 5 6 7 8 9 0 19 18 17 16 15

022015
WEP110215

Project Coordinator Aaron Carr
Art Director Terry Paulhus

Photo Credits
Every reasonable effort has been made to trace ownership and to obtain permission to reprint copyright material. The publishers would be pleased to have any errors or omissions brought to their attention so that they may be corrected in subsequent printings.

Weigl acknowledges Getty Images as its primary image supplier for this title.

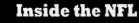

Chicago Bears

CONTENTS

Introduction

The Chicago Bears are one of the oldest and most storied franchises in the National Football League (NFL). Defined by grit, determination, and perseverance through adversity and harsh weather, the Bears have become a symbol of toughness, as beloved as they are feared.

The dominant force in the NFL before the NFL-American Football League (AFL) **merger** in 1970, the Bears have more **hall of famers** (27) than any other team in the league. Legends such as Dick Butkus and Mike Singletary forged the Bears' reputation through blood, sweat, and sacrifice. With the Bears' brightest stars dedicating themselves in this manner to the team, the team won more than games. They won the devotion of many fans.

Despite the popularity of the Cubs, White Sox, Blackhawks, and Bulls, Chicago is considered a football-first city.

Another reason the Bears enjoy such a loyal following is their long history. One of only two **charter members** left in the NFL, they have been playing hard-nosed football since the game's infancy. Long before this sport could bring its players fame and fortune, the Chicago Bears played through rain, sleet, snow and pain. They brought pride and glory to their Windy City.

Jay Cutler is the current starting quarterback of the Bears. He was traded to Chicago in 2009.

BEARS

Stadium Soldier Field

Division National Football Conference (NFC) North

Head coach Marc Trestman

Location Chicago, Illinois

NFL championships 1921, 1932, 1933, 1940, 1941, 1943, 1946, 1963, and 1985

Nicknames Da Bears, The Monsters of the Midway

25
Playoff Appearances

1
Super Bowl Championships

18
Division Championships

History

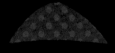

LONGEST RUNNING Besides the Bears, the only remaining **CHARTER MEMBER** of the NFL is the **ARIZONA CARDINALS.**

⊔ In 2008, ESPN named Red Grange the greatest football player of all time.

Formed in 1920, the Chicago Bears won their first NFL Championship in 1921. Four years later, they signed one of the greatest football players in the country, Red Grange. The Bears and Grange then went on a 19-game "barnstorming tour," playing teams all over the country and bringing national attention to the game of football. The 1930s and 1940s were good decades for the Bears. They started a **dynasty** by winning six NFL titles, including the NFL's first-ever Championship Game against the New York Giants in 1933. From 1940 to 1947, quarterback Sid Luckman led the Bears to five NFL Championship Games, four of which the Bears won. After the Bears' 73-0 defeat of the Washington Redskins in the 1940 NFL Championship, they were given the nickname "The Monsters of the Midway."

The Bears suffered through a long dry spell between 1947 and 1976, playing in only three **postseason** games. They won the championship in 1963, but were unable to build a consistent winner around star players Dick Butkus and Gale Sayers. The Bears won their first **Super Bowl** title in 1985 with a team that many consider the greatest in NFL history. With an innovative defense and a high-powered offense, the 1985 Bears' win-loss record was 18-1. They crushed the New England Patriots 46-10 in Super Bowl XX.

Dick Butkus was born in Chicago, and played his entire professional career for the Chicago Bears.

Chicago Bears

The Stadium

Soldier Field can currently seat 61,500 fans.

Constructed in 1924, Soldier Field is one of the oldest stadiums in the country. Although the original design of the stadium allowed for a maximum seating of just more than 74,000, it used to be possible to add additional seating for big sporting events.

Bears fans consistently brave the cold and the wind to support their team.

At the **annual** Army vs. Navy football game in 1926, more than 100,000 fans squeezed into the stadium. The following year, Soldier Field set the all-time collegiate attendance record when more than 123,000 fans attended a game between the University of Notre Dame and the University of Southern California.

Before playing their games at Soldier Field, the Bears called Wrigley Field home. Better known as the home of Chicago's beloved hard-luck baseball team, the Cubs, Wrigley Field housed the Bears for nearly 50 years. In 1971, a few years after the first Super Bowl, football's popularity was exploding. The NFL demanded that home teams play in stadiums capable of seating more than 50,000 fans, so the Bears moved into historic Soldier Field. Today, Soldier Field is the oldest home stadium in the NFL.

While catching a game at Soldier Field, fans gorge themselves on polish sausages and "Ditka Dogs," named for the famed Bears coach Mike Ditka.

Where They Play

CANADA

Washington **30**

Oregon

Montana

North Dakota

Minnesota

Lake Superior

Idaho

South Dakota

Wisconsin **23**

22

29

Nevada

Wyoming

Iowa

24

California **15**

Utah

14

Nebraska

Illinois

13

Colorado

Kansas

Missouri

UNITED STATES

31

16

Arizona

New Mexico

Oklahoma

Arkansas

32

17

Texas

Mississippi

Pacific Ocean

Louisiana

12

27

Alaska

0 500 Miles
0 500 km

Hawai'i

0 100 Miles
0 100 km

MEXICO

Gulf of Mexico

AMERICAN FOOTBALL CONFERENCE

EAST	NORTH	SOUTH	WEST
1 Gillette Stadium	5 FirstEnergy Stadium	9 EverBank Field	13 Arrowhead Stadium
2 MetLife Stadium	6 Heinz Field	10 LP Field	14 Sports Authority Field at Mile High
3 Ralph Wilson Stadium	7 M&T Bank Stadium	11 Lucas Oil Stadium	15 O.co Coliseum
4 Sun Life Stadium	8 Paul Brown Stadium	12 NRG Stadium	16 Qualcomm Stadium

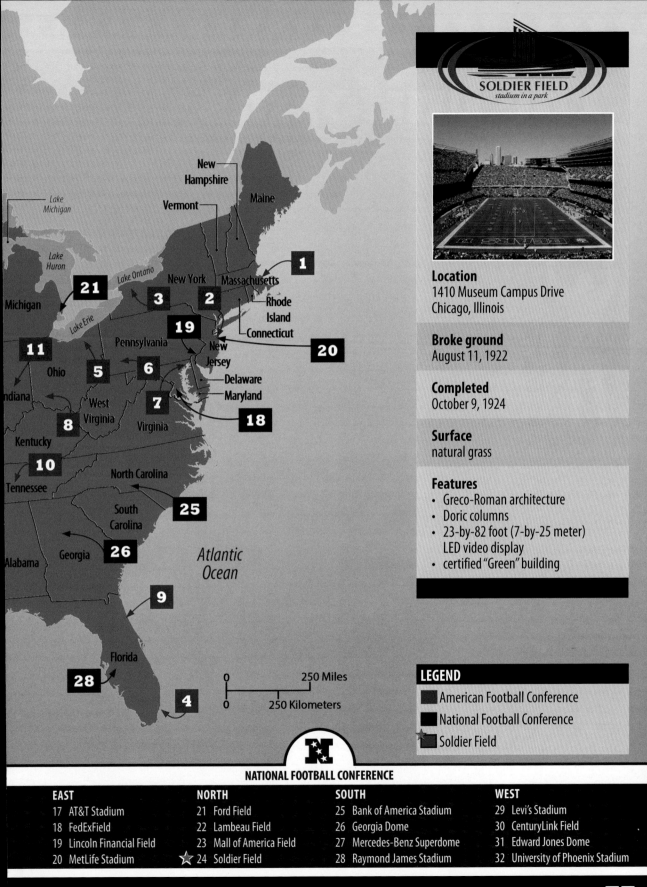

SOLDIER FIELD
stadium in a park

Location
1410 Museum Campus Drive
Chicago, Illinois

Broke ground
August 11, 1922

Completed
October 9, 1924

Surface
natural grass

Features
- Greco-Roman architecture
- Doric columns
- 23-by-82 foot (7-by-25 meter) LED video display
- certified "Green" building

LEGEND
American Football Conference
National Football Conference
Soldier Field

250 Miles
250 Kilometers

Lake Michigan
Lake Huron
Lake Ontario
Lake Erie

Michigan
New Hampshire
Maine
Vermont
New York
Massachusetts
Rhode Island
Connecticut
New Jersey
Pennsylvania
Ohio
Delaware
Maryland
Indiana
West Virginia
Virginia
Kentucky
North Carolina
South Carolina
Tennessee
Georgia
Alabama
Florida

Atlantic Ocean

NATIONAL FOOTBALL CONFERENCE

EAST	NORTH	SOUTH	WEST
17 AT&T Stadium	21 Ford Field	25 Bank of America Stadium	29 Levi's Stadium
18 FedExField	22 Lambeau Field	26 Georgia Dome	30 CenturyLink Field
19 Lincoln Financial Field	23 Mall of America Field	27 Mercedes-Benz Superdome	31 Edward Jones Dome
20 MetLife Stadium	☆ 24 Soldier Field	28 Raymond James Stadium	32 University of Phoenix Stadium

The Uniforms

THE BEARS have retired the jersey numbers of **14** of the TEAM'S GREATS, more than any other NFL franchise.

Captains such as Lance Briggs have a "C" on their jerseys to identify them as leaders.

The Bears' uniforms have gone through many changes during the Bears' 90-plus years. In their **inaugural** season, they wore blue jerseys with tan leather stripes sown into the fabric so ball carriers could better secure the football. In 1935, they changed the primary color from blue to orange with black stripes. By the 1950s, numbers were added to the sleeves to benefit television viewers. Their primary color was changed from black to navy blue.

In 1983, the initials "GSH" were added to the left sleeve in honor of the late "Papa Bear" George S. Halas, Bears' founder and primary head coach from 1920 to 1967.

In 2012, Nike redesigned the uniforms for all 32 NFL teams, allowing jerseys to stretch and more easily regain form.

The Helmets

To celebrate their
•75TH•
anniversary in 1994,
the Bears wore a
PLAIN BLUE
helmet with no "C"
on the side.

In a 2014 study,
research proved that
the design of football
helmets can affect
concussion risk.

Riddell

For their first 30-plus years as a team, the Bears wore a leather helmet. Over time, its color changed from reddish brown to blue to black. When plastic helmets were introduced into the league, the Bears kept things simple, did not have any **logo** on the helmet. However, in 1962, the team introduced the "Wishbone C" helmets. The team liked the design so much they decided to get rid of the black bear logo that had been a part of their identity since the beginning. The "Wishbone C" logo on their helmets has remained ever since.

In 1974, the Bears chose to change the color of their "Wishbone C" logo from white to orange with white trim. The Bears have **alternate jerseys** and helmets to wear on special occasions, but their primary helmets have gone unchanged for more than 40 years. Alternate logos include a black bear inside the "Wishbone C" and a bear's head.

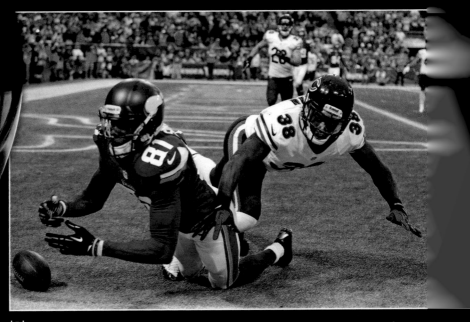

In addition to helmets, leg and shoulder pads are required to keep players safe.

The Coaches

33 The number of years since Marc Trestman had another job title besides football coach.

Trestman became a volunteer coach for the University of Miami in 1981.

◻ Marc Trestman bridges the gap between coach and teacher. "The beauty of this game is it draws people from everywhere, from different realities and different perceptions, but that can all be neutralized through respect," he said.

The Bears' sideline has been graced by some of the of the game's most memorable personalities. While discipline, grit, and toughness have defined the players, these qualities have been handed down by a series of coaches that set a very high standard. These men led by example and expected nothing less than their team's best effort every single game.

GEORGE HALAS

"Nobody who ever gave his best regretted it." These famous words of "Papa Bear" George Halas have been repeated time and again in locker rooms at every level of the sport. In his 39 years as their head coach, Halas led the Bears to 318 wins and eight NFL Championships.

MIKE DITKA

The coach of the famed 1985 Bears, Mike Ditka is a living legend. A five-time All Pro tight end for the Bears in his playing days, Ditka returned to coach the Bears in 1982. By the end of the 1984 season, he had transformed the team into a division winner. By the end of the 1985 season, he had coached perhaps the greatest Super Bowl champion in NFL history.

MARC TRESTMAN

Marc Trestman's leadership in the 2013 season filled Bears fans with hope. Under his guidance, the Bears transformed into an offensive threat, scoring the second-most points in the league (445). The 2013 Bears set team records in total yards (6,109), passing yards (4,450), and passing touchdowns (32).

The Mascot

Unlike real bears, Staley Da Bear does not hibernate during the winter. He is too busy getting the crowd pumped up before big games.

Since taking the NFL by storm in 2003, Staley Da Bear has not slowed down for one second. A five-time **Pro Bowl** mascot, Staley Da Bear is the owner of Bears' records for most T-shirts shot into the crowd (1,920) and most autographs signed (16,726), and may be approaching the world record for most high fives with more than 34 million! In addition to these achievements, Staley is a talented dancer who loves to show off his moves on the Bears sideline.

Staley Da Bear is named after the original name of the Chicago Bears franchise, the Decatur Staleys.

When Staley is not revving up the crowd, he finds other places to get his groove on. Among Staley's numerous public appearances, he loves to entertain Bears fans at schools, parties, and weddings.

Joining official mascot Staley D Bear in cheering duties is unofficial mascot "Bearman," a costumed season ticket holder who runs a Bears flag across the field when they score.

Legends of the Past

Many great players have suited up in the Bears' navy and orange. A few of them have become icons of the team and the city it represents.

Gale Sayers

Position Running Back
Seasons 7 (1965–1971)
Born May 30, 1943, in Wichita, Kansas

For five years with the Chicago Bears, Gale Sayers was one of the most dangerous offensive weapons in NFL history. As a Kansas Jayhawk, many believed that Sayers was the greatest open-field runner in the history of the college game. When he arrived in Chicago, nothing happened to alter that perception. In 1966, he had a league-leading 1,231 rushing yards, led the league in **yards from scrimmage** (1,678), and averaged a league-best 88 rushing yards per game. When knee injuries cut short his career, he continued to live and work in the Chicago area.

Dick Butkus

Dick Butkus is widely regarded as one of the greatest linebackers in NFL history. In fact, the "Butkus Award" is given each year to the best linebackers at the high school, collegiate, and professional levels.

Butkus was an eight-time Pro Bowler and six-time All Pro. In 1970, *Sports Illustrated* named Butkus "The Most Feared Man in the NFL." That season he demonstrated why he deserved that title, recording 216 tackles, three interceptions, two fumble recoveries, and one forced safety. He was elected to the Pro Football Hall of Fame in 1979.

Position Linebacker
Seasons 9 (1965–1973)
Born December 9, 1942, in Chicago, Illinois

Walter Payton

Mike Ditka described Walter Payton as the greatest football player he had ever seen, and an even greater human being. Known by fans as "Sweetness," Payton was a two-time NFL **Most Valuable Player (MVP)** and was a member of the 1985 Super Bowl-champion Bears. His signature style included a "stutter step" that caused defenders to miss and gave him an advantage against faster players. Always modest, Payton never celebrated touchdowns. He liked to hand the ball directly to teammates or the referee. When he retired, Payton was the NFL's all-time leader in career rushing yards, all-purpose yards, and touchdowns. He died tragically at the age of 45 from a rare liver disease.

Position Running Back
Seasons 13 (1975–1987)
Born July 25, 1954, in Columbia, Mississippi

Mike Singletary

Mike Singletary was influenced by linebackers like Dick Butkus. He was a key member of the "Monsters of the Midway" Bears defense. They led the franchise to its only Super Bowl title in 1985.

As durable as he was intense, Singletary missed only two games to injury during his 12-year career. Over the course of his career he was a 10-time Pro Bowler and two-time NFL Defensive Player of the Year. Singletary was given numerous nicknames, including "Samurai Mike" because of his intensity and focus. He was also called the "Minister of Defense" because he was a minister.

Position Running Back
Seasons 12 (1981–1992)
Born October 9, 1958, in Houston, Texas

Stars of Today

Today's Bears team is made up of many young, talented players who have proven that they are among the best players in the league.

Alshon Jeffery

A winner at every level, Alshon Jeffery starred on his high school basketball team. He led his team to four South Carolina state championships while going an incredible 80-0. Jeffery went on to become an All-American wide receiver at the University of South Carolina. After seeing limited playing time during his rookie season, Jeffery led the 2013 Bears in receiving yards (1,421), yards per catch (16), and made seven touchdown receptions. His 218 yards receiving yards against New Orleans in Week five broke a team record set back in 1952.

Position Wide Receiver
Seasons 2 (2012–2013)
Born February 14, 1990, in St. Matthews, South Carolina

Brandon Marshall

In 2012, Brandon Marshall crushed Bears' records for receptions (118) and receiving yards (1,508). It was the star receiver's sixth straight season with more than 1,000 receiving yards and the second time that he had caught more than 10 receiving touchdowns. Standing 6 feet, 4 inches and weighing 230 pounds, Marshall uses his size and strength to great advantage on the field. His strength, however, is not confined to the **gridiron**. Marshall has shown tremendous courage in speaking openly about changing the "culture of the NFL" that tolerates bullying.

Position Wide Receiver
Seasons 7 (2006–2013)
Born March 23, 1984, in Pittsburgh, Pennsylvania

Lance Briggs

In 2007, Bears star linebacker Brian Urlacher said that he was willing to take a pay cut in order to keep Briggs in Chicago. This proved to the team and fans alike how important Lance Briggs was to the team. A seven-time Pro Bowler, Briggs has been at the heart of the Bears defense since 2003. He has registered more than 100 tackles eight times, collected 15 interceptions and forced 15 fumbles. In 2012, Briggs tied a career best with 11 pass deflections. For 11 seasons with Chicago, Briggs has been a **centerpiece** of the Bears' defense, a true leader of the "Monsters of the Midway."

Position Linebacker
Seasons 11 (2003–2013)
Born November 12, 1980, in Los Angeles, California

Jay Cutler

The Bears signed Jay Cutler in 2009. Before finding Cutler, the Bears had tried out 12 different quarterbacks since the beginning of the 2000 season. With Cutler on the roster, their search was over. In Cutler, the Bears had a man with a strong arm and an ability to put up huge numbers. In his final season with the Denver Broncos, Cutler had passed for more than 4,500 yards. He did not waste any time in showing Bears fans what they had been missing. In his first season as a Bear, Cutler threw for 26 touchdowns and 3,666 yards.

Position Quarterback
Seasons 8 (2006–2013)
Born April 29, 1983, in Columbus, Georgia

All-Time Records

1,508 Single-Season Receiving Yards

In 2012, Brandon Marshall set the Bears' all-time mark for single-season receiving yards and made a franchise-record 118 receptions.

16,726 Career Rushing Yards

Walter Payton's career rushing yards were the top mark in the NFL at the time of his retirement. "Sweetness" currently ranks number two on the all-time list.

318
All-time Coaching Wins

George Halas' 318 coaching wins are the most in the history of the franchise and the second most in NFL history.

14,686
Career Passing Yards

Sid Luckman, who led the Bears to four NFL Championships during his 12-year career, is also the Bears' all-time leader with 137 touchdown passes.

2,440
Single-season All-Purpose Yards

Gale Sayers set a then-NFL record for all-purpose yards in 1966. Sayers gained 1,231 rushing yards, 447 receiving yards, and 762 return yards.

Timeline

Throughout the team's history, the Chicago Bears have had many memorable events that have become defining moments for the team and its fans.

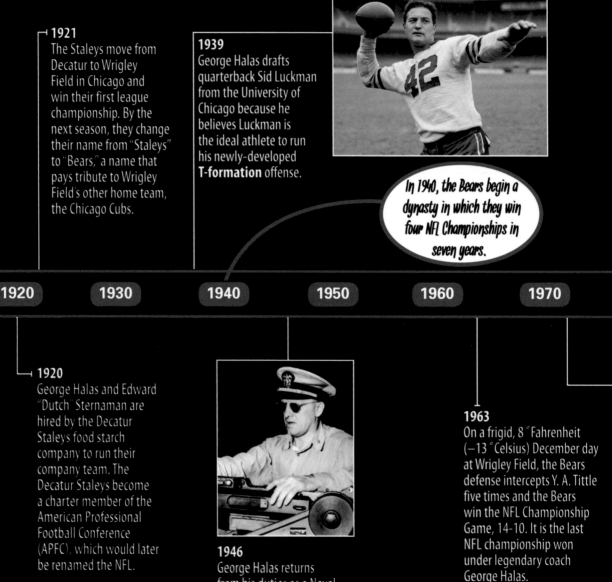

1921
The Staleys move from Decatur to Wrigley Field in Chicago and win their first league championship. By the next season, they change their name from "Staleys" to "Bears," a name that pays tribute to Wrigley Field's other home team, the Chicago Cubs.

1939
George Halas drafts quarterback Sid Luckman from the University of Chicago because he believes Luckman is the ideal athlete to run his newly-developed **T-formation** offense.

In 1940, the Bears begin a dynasty in which they win four NFL Championships in seven years.

| 1920 | 1930 | 1940 | 1950 | 1960 | 1970 |

1920
George Halas and Edward "Dutch" Sternaman are hired by the Decatur Staleys food starch company to run their company team. The Decatur Staleys become a charter member of the American Professional Football Conference (APFC), which would later be renamed the NFL.

1946
George Halas returns from his duties as a Naval Captain in World War II to lead the Bears to their final title of the decade.

1963
On a frigid, 8°Fahrenheit (−13°Celsius) December day at Wrigley Field, the Bears defense intercepts Y. A. Tittle five times and the Bears win the NFL Championship Game, 14-10. It is the last NFL championship won under legendary coach George Halas.

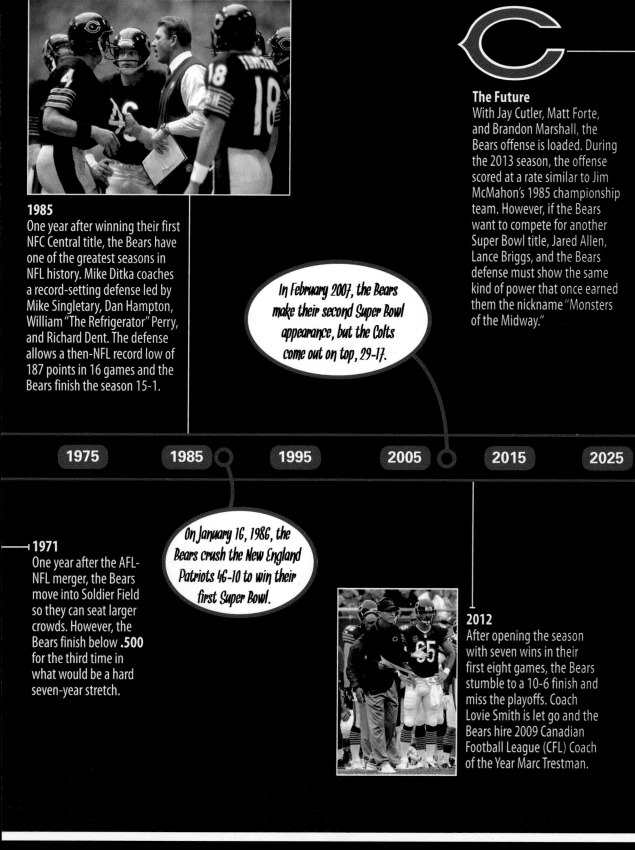

1985
One year after winning their first NFC Central title, the Bears have one of the greatest seasons in NFL history. Mike Ditka coaches a record-setting defense led by Mike Singletary, Dan Hampton, William "The Refrigerator" Perry, and Richard Dent. The defense allows a then-NFL record low of 187 points in 16 games and the Bears finish the season 15-1.

The Future
With Jay Cutler, Matt Forte, and Brandon Marshall, the Bears offense is loaded. During the 2013 season, the offense scored at a rate similar to Jim McMahon's 1985 championship team. However, if the Bears want to compete for another Super Bowl title, Jared Allen, Lance Briggs, and the Bears defense must show the same kind of power that once earned them the nickname "Monsters of the Midway."

In February 2007, the Bears make their second Super Bowl appearance, but the Colts come out on top, 29-17.

| 1975 | 1985 | 1995 | 2005 | 2015 | 2025 |

On January 16, 1986, the Bears crush the New England Patriots 46-10 to win their first Super Bowl.

1971
One year after the AFL-NFL merger, the Bears move into Soldier Field so they can seat larger crowds. However, the Bears finish below **.500** for the third time in what would be a hard seven-year stretch.

2012
After opening the season with seven wins in their first eight games, the Bears stumble to a 10-6 finish and miss the playoffs. Coach Lovie Smith is let go and the Bears hire 2009 Canadian Football League (CFL) Coach of the Year Marc Trestman.

Write a Biography

Life Story

A person's life story can be the subject of a book. This kind of book is called a biography. Biographies often describe the lives of people who have achieved great success. These people may be alive today, or they may have lived many years ago. Reading a biography can help you learn more about a great person.

Get the Facts

Use this book, and research in the library and on the Internet, to find out more about your favorite Bear. Learn as much about this player as you can. What position does he play? What are his statistics in important categories? Has he set any records? Also, be sure to write down key events in the person's life. What was his childhood like? What has he accomplished off the field? Is there anything else that makes this person special or unusual?

Use the Concept Web

A concept web is a useful research tool. Read the questions in the concept web on the following page. Answer the questions in your notebook. Your answers will help you write a biography.

Concept Web

Adulthood
- Where does this individual currently reside?
- Does he or she have a family?

Your Opinion
- What did you learn from the books you read in your research?
- Would you suggest these books to others?
- Was anything missing from these books?

Childhood
- Where and when was this person born?
- Describe his or her parents, siblings, and friends.
- Did this person grow up in unusual circumstances?

Accomplishments off the Field
- What is this person's life's work?
- Has he or she received awards or recognition for accomplishments?
- How have this person's accomplishments served others?

Write a Biography

Help and Obstacles
- Did this individual have a positive attitude?
- Did he or she receive help from others?
- Did this person have a mentor?
- Did this person face any hardships?
- If so, how were the hardships overcome?

Accomplishments on the Field
- What records does this person hold?
- What key games and plays have defined his or her career?
- What are his or her stats in categories important to his or her position?

Work and Preparation
- What was this person's education?
- What was his or her work experience?
- How does this person work; what is the process he or she uses?

Trivia Time

Take this quiz to test your knowledge of the Chicago Bears. The answers are printed upside-down under each question.

1 Which Bear was the first NFL player ever to return the opening kickoff in a Super Bowl?

A. Devin Hester

2 The award for the nation's best linebacker in high school, college, and the pros is named for which Chicago Bear?

A. Dick Butkus

3 How many NFL Championships do the Bears own?

A. Nine

4 Which Chicago Bear was nicknamed "Sweetness"?

A. Walter Payton

5 Which Bears player was the franchise's founder?

A. George Halas

6 Who is the Bears' unofficial mascot?

A. Bearman

7 Which Bears running back led the league in all-purpose yards for three straight seasons in the 1960s?

A. Gale Sayers

8 Which former Bears tight end coached them to their first Super Bowl title?

A. Mike Ditka

9 Which Bears defender was nicknamed "The Minister of Defense"?

A. Mike Singletary

10

A. Wrigley Field

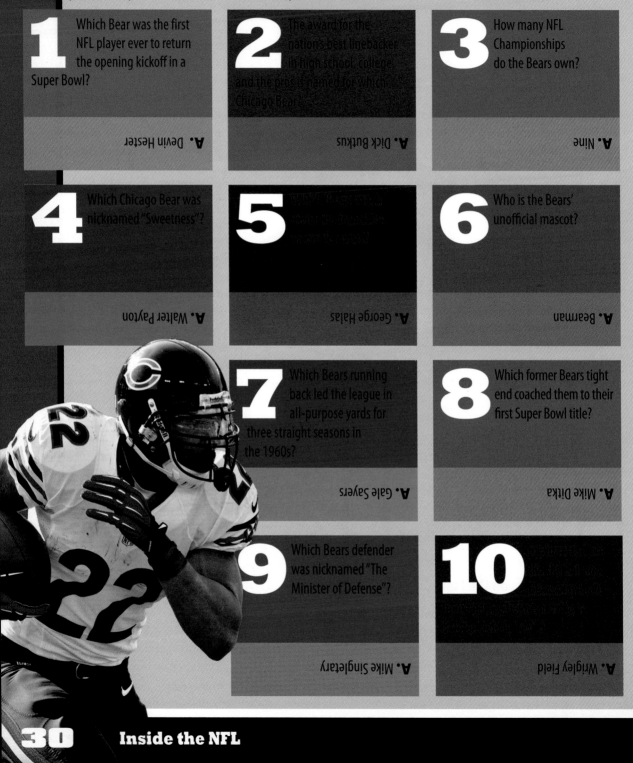

Key Words

.500 season: when a team wins and loses an equal number of games. In the NFL, an 8-8 record constitutes a .500 season

all-purpose yards: also referred to as combined net yards, all-purpose yards are a statistic that measures total yardage gained on receptions, runs from scrimmage, punt returns, and kickoff returns

alternate jerseys: a jersey that sports teams may wear in games instead of their home or away uniforms

annual: something that occurs once a year

centerpiece: a player intended to be the focus of attention

charter members: original or founding members of an organization

dynasty: a team that wins a series of championships in a short period of time

gridiron: a field for football, marked with regularly spaced parallel lines

hall of famers: players judged to be outstanding in a sport

inaugural: marking the beginning of an institution, activity, or period of office

logo: a symbol that stands for a team or organization

merger: a combination of two things, especially companies, into one

Most Valuable Player (MVP): the player judged to be most valuable to his team's success

postseason: a sporting event that takes place after the end of the regular season

Pro Bowl: the annual all-star game for NFL players pitting the best players in the National Football Conference against the best players in the American Football Conference

Super Bowl: the NFL's annual championship game between the winning team from the NFC and the winning team from the AFC

"T-formation": a T-shaped offensive formation, with the halfbacks and fullback positioned in a line parallel to the line of scrimmage

yards from scrimmage: the total of rushing yards and receiving yards

Index

Log on to www.av2books.com

AV² by Weigl brings you media enhanced books that support active learning. Go to www.av2books.com, and enter the special code found on page 2 of this book. You will gain access to enriched and enhanced content that supplements and complements this book. Content includes video, audio, weblinks, quizzes, a slide show, and activities.

AV² Online Navigation

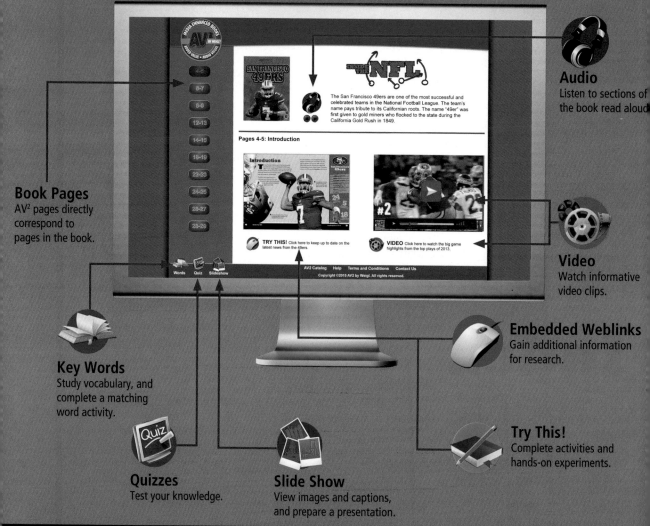

Audio
Listen to sections of the book read aloud

Book Pages
AV² pages directly correspond to pages in the book.

Video
Watch informative video clips.

Key Words
Study vocabulary, and complete a matching word activity.

Embedded Weblinks
Gain additional information for research.

Quizzes
Test your knowledge.

Slide Show
View images and captions, and prepare a presentation.

Try This!
Complete activities and hands-on experiments.

AV² was built to bridge the gap between print and digital. We encourage you to tell us what you like and what you want to see in the future.

Sign up to be an AV² Ambassador at www.av2books.com/ambassador.